Dear Reader,

*I hate to admit it, but I have finally reached middle age, or to be more honest, I am just on the edge of the cliff from being "old"; at least in my grandchildren's eyes. And who sees clearer than a bunch of preschoolers with virgin honesty that has not yet been corrupted by watching us adults? No one I have yet to meet in **my** travels, anyway.*

*For most of my adult life I have been writing about life around me as I see it. First as a CBS affiliate anchorperson and then as an author and playwright. And for several years now I have been writing an ezine, **Read Between My Lines**, about everyday living and how to make the most of it.*

Come along with me as I share a pot pourri of thoughts on life as I see it.

Sandra Hart

1

By Sandra Hart

Quiche the Sausage Dog
Places Within My Heart
Behind The Mirror Parts I and II
Behind The Magic Mirror
Death Certificate
Tit For Tat This And That
Lucy's Line
Marshell's Surprise ·

What Was I Thinking

Library of Congress Control Number: 2006910121
ISBN 978-0-9715525-2-4

Published by
Myartisansway Press
10 Ballinswood Road Suite 3
Atlantic Highlands, New Jersey 07716
www.sandrahart.net
www.sandrahart.mobi

Printed in the United States of America
Published in 2007

What Was I Thinking.

Read Between My Lines:

What Was I Thinking?

By

Sandra Hart

What Was I Thinking

For my children Brett, Alison and Emerson who have inspired much of my writings.
To my devoted husband Arthur who always has been my best cheerleader.
Thank you all for your unconditional love and support.
Special appreciation to Bill Thompson who has been my best literary champion throughout the years.

What Was I Thinking

Forgive the mistakes that are always there in spite of a thousand editorial eyes.

What Was I Thinking

Prologue

I am at my happiest when I am with my family or when I am creating. And it doesn't hurt to have a water view, as well!

As much as I enjoy being in the public arena, entertaining, lecturing and helping other people, I was born a very introspective person.

For some reason I have not always been able to comfortably share my own deepest thoughts and feelings, even with my closest friends and family. Perhaps that is why writing so comfortable for me. What I feel, what I think becomes a fountain when put on paper.

As a young girl with an older brother who was always off on his own with his friends, I learned to use my creativity to entertain myself. Being able to put my thoughts and feelings down has always been joyful to me.

Read Between My Lines is a compilation of some of my thoughts that I would like to share with you.

What Was I Thinking

What Was I thinking

The blank pages you will find from time to time in this book is
for your own use in jotting down you own personal thoughts
during your reading.

Sandra Hart

What Was I Thinking

"Aging has made me internally fearless, except when I have to expose my external shell."

Fear Of Flashing

When I got back from Florida this spring, I went shopping with my daughter and 11 year-old grandson. It was a humbling experience to say the least and not the homecoming I had anticipated.

"Nana," he said in his trendy Star Wars T- shirt, "we've gotta' get you out of those 'grandma jeans". No one wears those high-waist, straight things anymore except old people. You need to get more modern 'cause your face looks young."

Both flattered and shattered at the same time, I knew my little darling had my best interest at heart so I tried not to drop dead from humiliation right there in the middle of the mall floor. These days who wants to walk around with a grandma that really looks like one? It just isn't cool.

So I was reluctantly lead to American Eagle Outfitters to get in touch with my 'younger self'. With a new understanding of 'reality bites', after numerous trials I finally pushed, pulled and squeezed into just the right 'young Nana' hip- hugging, flare-leg American Eagles. My white cotton Nana underwear was sticking up about two inches above my new look, for all the world to see.

Independent soul that I have always thought myself to be, I never thought I would become a slave to fashion trends, but here I sit, typing in my tight jeans, legs thrust straight forward under the desk and trying not to flash my Shih Tzu sitting on the floor behind me. Somehow I just can't get used to feeling a constant draft in places usually covered. My fear of flashing the world has been overcome by my fear of growing old in my grandson's eyes.

Who would have figured?

The acceptance and patience of our pets make them our teachers.

The Family Bed

As my rheumatologist once put it "humans weren't designed to walk upright."

It's hard for me to get out of bed in the morning with the creeks and cranks that come with life experience...to put it honestly, of living into the arthritis age.

The problem is that our pets Harley and Jengo enjoy our warm bed as much as my husband and I. Now if these were our little children I would embrace their wanting to snuggle up to Mother and Dad once in awhile. But they are a Shih Tzu and a tabby cat. Shame on us.

Never in my wildest dreams did I think I would be sharing my bed with animals (other than my husband). But we're old softies, so there they sleep, between my legs, on my feet or any spot they can stake out for themselves before Arthur and I even get between the sheets.

Having to go to the bathroom in the middle of the night is impossible and in the morning I fake sleeping later than they, so that their absence has unpinned my legs and my circulation is begins to return.

We've tried heartlessly locking them out of the room, but their plaintive whines and cries are more than we can bear, so we give in time after time, destroying all resolve to ignore the noise on the other side of our door.

So I'm stuck with my morning limp to the coffee pot as the Jengo caresses my ankles in his best effort to charm his way to be fed before I can pour myself something that will relax my animal induced paralysis.

There has to be a payback somewhere for all of this in doggie heaven. I'm waiting!

Aging Gracefully. Who Says?

I've learned a new meaning for 'sweet' from my grandson. To me "sweet' has always meant the stuff that packed the pounds onto my hips, the taste of root beer or the look on my little girls' faces when they wanted something from me. But today it seems that 'sweet' has replaced 'cool' in hip teenage vernacular. So when I think of aging gracefully, if there is such a thing, I say 'sweet'.

The other day I recalled the comedian Jackie Gleason's famous line as his character Ralph in *The Honeymooners*, "How sweet it is!" To me that always meant things were darn good. So maybe this current tweaking of the meaning of 'sweet' is not too far from

Ralph's gleeful proclamations years ago when life was rockin' with Alice.

All of this thought pattern continued when I recently picked up at my local Barnes & Noble a copy of Dr. Andrew Weil's new book, "Healthy Aging." According to Dr. Weil we all begin aging from the time of birth,

He quotes the words of an Eastern philosopher, *"The sun at noon is the sun declining; the person born is the person dying."*

Aging is really not reversible. But on the positive side, his message is clear.

At any age it is important to learn how to live in appropriate ways in order to maximize health and happiness. That really should be an essential goal for all of us.

Children at times can be both joy and the backside of heaven.

Help Me, Dr. Spock!

So what! If I wasn't perfect, get over it, kids! I don't know about you, but no one gave me a text book on raising children. Dr. Spock's baby guide was all the reference I had at the time when I needed a much better "how-to" to get me through the first eighteen years, at least.

All I can say is, I did the best I could with what tools I had to work with. But evidentially that wasn't good enough, or at least that is what my children claim. Oh, the mistakes I made according to them would fill a book that would take me a year to read. But in spite of all their complaints, I think they still love me most of the time.

I have spoken to enough parents in my travels to know that I am not an island and that many children take the easy path of blaming Mom on all of their adult troubles and choices.

On a personal level, this used to bother me a lot, because I really did try my best as a single mom. But it was not until my own children became parents, that they have become more forgiving of my parenting skills.

If I made some wrong parenting choices along the way, I have to console myself that I did more right than wrong. Each of my children are honest and caring parents and hard-working professionals that continue to give back to the world in a positive way.

They are not just walking through this life without purpose and meaning. I kind of hope that is because of my parenting skills and the image of me they saw growing up.

Time For a Facelift

Time for a facelift. Over the years the fifties knotty pine walls and green cabinets in my 1950's kitchen have been covered up with white paint more than once, but in my recent menopause fever, burgundy cabinets and a sky blue ceiling, accenting a new dress of white walls kept swirling around in my head. I could blame my color boldness on Prempro withdrawal, or on Sharon Osborne's hair, but I had to admit I had neglected this space in our house for too long.

As the painters went about making over my old friend, I decided to clean out her drawers. Mother always told me to wear clean underwear in case I was ever in an accident, why should my kitchen be any different?

I decided to clean out her drawers. Crock pots, old blenders with cracked glass tops, my Sunbeam mixer with just one beater left that my brother and sister-in-law gave me for a wedding present a gad-zillion years ago - all went to Gadget Heaven, or wherever no-longer-useful and imperfect kitchen things go.

Then came the 'junk drawer' where everything and anything that we never knew what to do with for decades landed. Throw it in, close the drawer, and it disappeared. How great is that! What magic 'junk drawers' possess. Things in there sometimes disappeared forever.

Our junk drawer had various screwdrivers, old hammers, rusty old bread ties, nails, tons of keys to nowhere, teak pegs from our Smith & Hawkin garden benches, old rubber bands that had stuck to the bottom of the drawer, a million tacks and assorted rusty screws also glued to the bottom of the drawer by the open can of cement glue that must have been twenty years old and a toothless grade school picture of my now 40 year old child. I also found two round rubber lid openers with barely legible names of businesses that were once upon a time so kind to give to us.

After hours of throwing out, scraping and cleaning in preparation of a fresher appearance, the drawer was painted, then lined with floral paper. In slipped into their new home perfectly folded new tea towels in coordinated colors to match my good friend's new dress. The junk gone, new colorful rugs, and the magical colors make my heart sing each time I pass by the kitchen.

The other day, though, as I was trying to open that large jar of artichoke hearts we bought at our local super-duper Costco store, I opened the junk drawer and reached for my round rubber lid 'helper-offer' and saw my beautiful tea towels starring so perfectly back at me. Oh well, who wanted artichoke hearts anyway? Yogurt anyone?

What Was I Thinking

Music helps me see the truth better than reading glasses.

Music Maestro Please

I would like to explore music and its place in our lives. A few of my friends have no interest in music and can take it or leave it, but music has always been an important part of my life.

As a young child in Ohio I remember lying across my parents big bed on Saturday afternoons near the small wooden radio listening to operas coming from the Metropolitan Opera House in New York City. I never missed a performance. That exposure was the first I can mark as the beginning of my love of music...all music.

Now, having recently traveled around the world, I was for the first time in years cognizant of and intimately exposed to various types of music native to diverse cultures. So whether or not music just has to be an integral part of your daily life, think about this.

In Fiji we were treated to an ancient tribal ceremony with primitive vocal melodies accompanied by native percussion instruments imitating the movement of conflict, tropical winds and breezes.

The Japanese are very polite, ritualistic with a sense of calm and order about them. I found the traditional music of Japan even, ritualistic, soothing and quite beautiful. Their music is indeed indicative of their culture.

The Chinese and East Indian music is as kinetic as their unique societies. Again, the roots of the native music seem to grow from the energy of their peoples.

If we in the universe could only recognize our united love of music and acknowledge the importance of music and use it as a common denominator and as a healing tool to advance world peace. Now that is a dream worth aiming toward,.

"I've learned from experience that the greater part of our happiness or misery depends on our dispositions and not our circumstances." Martha Washington

Remembering Darth Vader

Several years ago I was a member of a theater ensemble in New York. One of the actresses in our troupe, that in spite of some bumps in life always had the ability to see the humorous side to life.

She had attended the Royal Academy of Dramatic Arts in England with good friend Diana Riggs. Through the ensuing years she had a respectable theater career, experienced the unthinkable loss of her only son and eventually, when I met her she was in her second marriage.

Working in an ensemble brings everyone together for many hours; finding plays, reading plays, rehearsing plays and rehearsing, rehearsing, rehearsing. If you are lucky, all of this togetherness does mimic a family atmosphere, therefore after awhile very little becomes sacred and our private lives are an open book to one another. When my friend started calling her husband Darth Vadar I suspected that something was amiss within her outward bliss.

We would always have a shameless giggle during our backstage nervousness waiting for our cues when she would address him that way. But hidden under her humor it didn't take a rocket scientist to see she was struggling to stay in her marriage.

Well, years have passed and Darth Vadar went his own way after my friend could no longer tolerate his dark moments. She eventually moved to Los Angeles, and she continues to live her single life successfully with great gusto and humor.

For her, the end of a relationship brought new opportunities to enrich her life. She didn't sit down and feel sorry for herself or mourn her relationship choice. She got up a bit older and wiser, dusted herself off and began again. She didn't hesitate to take her own leap of discovery into a new life and landed firmly on her own two feet. To this day, I have never had a conversation with her that she wasn't able to turn a bump in the road into a field of flowers. Her positive attitude toward life and the detours or prizes that have come along with those decisions has always been an inspiration to me. She has always been willing to jump into life with both feet and has, in the end, always come out a winner. She has never been willing to 'go over to the dark side.'

What Was I Thinking

Anyone Have A Clothespin?

There is one universal odor that I believe everyone at least once in their lifetime has experienced. Either driving along the highway, walking outdoors or brought home by your wiggly-tailed-four-footed best friend. The awful breath-taking perfume from a black and white bushy-tailed member of the weasel family that has switched into survival mode-the skunk. Up until now, I believed that the skunk's fetid defensive fluid was the most foul odor on this earth. It took my 12 pound Shih Tzu to prove me wrong once again.

Harley and my husband took a morning romp along the beach and arrived back home without having to give a 'ho, we're home.' I could smell Harley a mile away.

"He rolled in some rotten fish entrals," my husband

casually remarked, "I think he needs a bath."

Never mind that I just bathed him yesterday. I was not about to repeat that ritual again so soon. Armed with the miracle fabric freshener Fabreeze I chased Harley around the house until I was able to spritz him squarely. The moisture in the Fabreeze made the odor even worse. Having no other alternative than to cruelly banish our small pup to the garage for a week, I reluctantly bathed him three times in Tea Tree oil shampoo. The odor still lingered.

At my wits end and resigned to smelling foul fish odor for a few days, I vengefully put Harley next to my husband out on the deck to dry when my eye caught the bottle of Avon's Skin So Soft that I keep on the patio table as a mosquito repellant. What will there be to lose I thought as I doused poor Harley with the strong herbal oil and rubbed it into his coat. An Avon miracle! Like magic the offending odor was gone.

Leave it to the old line cosmetics company AVON to produce a bath oil that smoothes skin, repels mosquitoes, and neutralizes the smell of rotten fish entrails. HUMM...I wonder how much Avon stock is selling for these days?

It's Not Easy Being Green

Sometimes it's a tough life when you are born with an all-consuming-where-did-this-come-from-I-can't-help-myself creative gene. In my own little artistic nest, whenever I am feeling the roller coaster effect of a creative life, I often think of my old friend Kermit the Frog to get my feet back on the ground. Kermit's truism has kept me going many a day and helped me realize that I am not alone. ***"It's not easy being green."***

If you just ***have*** to follow your creative heart, the life of an artisan can be very rewarding when we see those creations, or extensions of ourselves, go from the first embryonic inspiration to it's completion. And no matter how much our works please us, the downside is that creativity is very ***subjective*** and often the artisan's work is open to critical review, with the pendulum of appreciation swinging both ways.

Therefore, it is very important that we create for

ourselves and our own fulfillment and, in the process, if others are touched by our works, then we have reached the pinnacle of creative gratification. And if we get paid for doing it, that's icing on the cake.

I think I wrote my first poem in the first grade, something about dew drops in the grass, as I remember it. Even then, I never missed an opportunity to write and perform little dramas with my childhood friends. Living on a farm and later in an industrial town in the Ohio Valley during the 50's, I certainly was not exposed outside of my home to as much creativity as those living in more cosmopolitan urban areas, but my need to create has never subsided and is still a driving force within me.

Although, while considering myself as one of the fortunate few who have been given the chance to be employed in several areas of creativity from time to time, I have never lost touch with artisans who have crossed my path, more talented than I, who are content with the passion of the act of creation as a whole in itself.

This is a lesson I'll never forget and one I hope will keep me loving the art of creating just for the personal joy of it.

Finding Your Melody

Each of us was born with a song, unique to us alone. Sometimes it takes a lifetime to discover our voices, our song, but the less you search for an answer to 'why', and the more you reach down deep inside to understand your song and let it happen naturally, the 'why' becomes unnecessary and almost elementary.

I was fortunate to achieve career success early in my life and I thought for sure that that was to be my life's song. At least is was always what I dreamed of. But, it turns out to be that it was not my best song. My life and events in my life changed my song. The song that I am now singing is not full of answers, but one of hope and positive re-enforcement to others. This is my life and that is my song.

My next door neighbor in Florida is a young woman who radiates beauty inside and out. Her positive, giving attitude and kindness is her song and her joy of life gives me a lift every time I speak with her. She has found her composition in compassion and in doing so has been given many of life's rewards. It is her joy of song that makes her so special to all she meets.

Your life has a song that you should share with others, too. Don't look for it, or wonder why, but just as our feathered friends do, sing because your song is there.

You Are All You've Got

Most of us know how to love others, but how good are we at taking care of the love of You, your most important self? From the beginning of time, women have long been caretakers of others and not so much of ourselves. Of course, there have been exceptions, (i.e. Samson's Delilah who only feigned protecting her man and also several Shakespearean women I can think of) but the maternal instinct runs long and deep for most of us women.

My name is a derivation of Alexander and means protector of men. In my lifetime, unfortunately I have been guilty of living up to this meaning of my given name. Guilty not in the sense that it was a totally misguided mission, but it was an embodiment of my character that caused my own self-esteem much harm for a long time. A good life, a worthwhile life does not always have to mean constant self-sacrifice.

It took me a long time to understand that I could give and keep at the same time. As the Fox's News Channel boasts, "fair and balanced." I do know that is is easier said than done, but this is what we should be aiming for if we want to set our sails for a happy and complete life. I'm not too sure she was the best role model in her time, but the late singer Janis Joplin once said something that rings true with me. She said, "Don't compromise yourself. You are all you've got."

Too Soon

Somehow I took it for granted that she would always be there, compassionately patching up my wounds of body and soul and gently lending me her loving shoulder for comfort when I needed it; her warm arms for that reassuring hug when I lost the spelling bee; my mirror of self-worth when I didn't get asked to my junior prom. She was my lifelong friend, cahampion and confidant. Her door was always open to me and mine to her. She was my best friend, my mother, and I miss her.

A year has passed since Mother flew away to something better, a more perfect existence we are to believe, but time seems to have stood still for me since I receided that phone call from the doctor relaying the news to me that Mother had died.

He tried to soften the blow by well-meaning words, but somehow it was not enough. It was too soon. I was ot ready to let go of her. Not yet.Not just yet. Certainly I would have the joy of a few more years to

41

share the wonders of her great-grandchildren with her, to take her to have her hair done, to sneak off together like two school gorl playing hooky to an afternoon movie, shring a big bag of buttery popcorn.

Mother and I have a long history of movies together. During the 1940's, movies were a wonderful escape for everyone torn by the hardships and loss of a country at war.

When she would take me to the movies, she said I would constantly run up and try toget on the stage. I remember so desperately wanting to be a part of that wonderful life I saw on the screen. She would hold me securely on her lap to prevent me from running up the aisle to join the life I saw before me.

I eventually learned the difference between reality and the fantasy of the movie screen and mother finally allowed me the privilege of a seat of my own next to her in the dark wonderland of the theater.

My mother always was the best champion of my dreams.To Mother, her children were her reward in this life. We were her Pulitzer Prize, her Academy Award. The joy of watching us achieve our dreams, the dreams she defended, in her eyes, was the ultimate prize.

To Leap, Or Not To Leap

Author's note: *If you have read my book "Behind The Magic Mirror", you know I have faced the worst of challenges squarely, but there are other life events that may not be life-threatening, but are very real and immobilizing for many of us.)*

One of the biggest problems we can encounter when we consider making changes to our life is that brick wall we can't seem to get over. Even though the changes we want to make will bring more happiness by considerably enhancing our lives, self- doubt and fear of leaping over that wall to the other side will still try and stop us in our tracks.

Why does this happen?

Now that's a million dollar question, isn't it? To leap is not only the action of leaping, but it is to hopefully hit the ground somewhere better than where you are at that moment. You can't always gage it perfectly, but in the action of doing, you must not

43

forget to realize that taking the leap is nothing short of an act of courage.

Realistically, most of us don't get epiphanies. We only get a faint whisper, perhaps just the slightest of urges. My big whisper, one that changed my life forever came not from within me, but from my mother years ago when she convinced me to audition for Romper Room. So fearful and so sure that I didn't have any of the qualifications for the television show, I was focused on 'what's next' instead of what was first. I was afraid to believe in myself by holding myself accountable for the opportunity I was being given.

My mother's whisper taught me that there is nothing more brave than filtering out the chatter (in my own head) that kept telling me that I was someone I was not. She taught me that there is nothing more genuine than breaking away from the chorus to learn the sound of my own voice. Taking that first leap was nothing short of positive belief in myself. Needless to say, I got the job and it did change my life forever.

I don't know about you but the ultimate feeling I want before I breathe my last is that I didn't take advantage of opportunities because I gave in to my refusal to leap forward. My almost missing a life altering opportunity was my wake-up call that shook me out of my complacency. What will yours be? It is up to you to take your own leap of discovery into a new life

The Love Affair

began when you took me for a rainy afternoon stroll
when you babysat me and let me eat all the cookies
when you threw my hat into the wind
after you sent my mother daisies
because I could hear your tiny voice
when you taught me to drive
when you held me through the night
and I realized that love wears many faces

What Was I Thinking

If Only

If only my husband had not let Skipper, our sweet little Chihuahua, out of the house, he would still be here. If only I had taken the time to fetch the step-ladder, I wouldn't have fallen. Each of us has our own personal lists of "if onlys" and we spend too much time with regrets and wishing that our "if onlys" come true.

One thing is sure, we can't change the past. "If only" you could get married. "If only" you could be thinner, or get that new job you will be happy, will not necessarily fix your life or result in the happiness that we so crave.

Happiness is accepting the reality of today and

working to change those things that are making you feel that your happiness is being denied. Make a list of the circumstances that you want to change in your life and then right next to that actions that will help you achieve your goal.

For instance, make of list of goals you can achieve to make that happen. One step at a time.

But remember it is so important to not miss the everyday simple joys of 'in the moment' happiness along the way. A hug from your child or spouse, a fresh bouquet of flowers, a night out at the movies, listening to your favorite music. It is important that small moments of happiness are savored and not swallowed up by future dreams of "if onlys". The simple secret of happiness is enjoying each day and finding something special along the way within those 24 hours.

So You Want To Be A Writer

Here is a 60 second lesson on writing. They say everyone has a story in them. I think that is true. Whether it is a memoir or a work of fiction, if you have the desire, all you need is discipline. Every story has a beginning, a middle and an end. Here is how to begin.

Write two pages of text a day, mornings or evenings, according to your time and creative peak. If you stay to this schedule faithfully, in 365 days (one year) you will have an unedited 730 page manuscript, or one page a day will give you a 365 page manuscript.

What Was I Thinking

Don't Call Us, We'll Call You

Last week I had several 'do as I say, not as I do' days. One would think that after all of these years in the acting arena, that I would by now be immune to rejection. NOT! Sometimes, I face it like a champ, but other times I am a real wimp and crawl into a corner to lick my wounds.

Nothing is beneath me; incontinence ads, arthritis medication print jobs and hiding my cellulite in a sarong for a Coppertone spray commercial. Ah, the angst of an aging actress who will do just about anything to keep working.

The other day I got a call-back (second audition) for a part in a movie (means the director really likes you!) A small character part as a daycare worker with a half-dozen lines. Well, to make a long sad story short, in between my first audition and second, my agent forgot to inform me that the director decided he wanted this character to be like his high school gym teacher, otherwise noted in the new script "butchy."

When I arrived at the call-back, the other two women reading for the part were short, muscular with hairy arms and wearing gym trunks, I knew I was dead in the water, but I was determined to be the best I could be. I am many things, but with my long red hair and curves, masculine is a real stretch.

It was no surprise when the casting director raised his eyebrow when I walked into the room. "The director loved your reading and the call-back was before the change in character direction. "But didn't your agent tell you?" I heard silent screams within his head.

Real trouper that I am I did my best to do a 'butchy' reading and for the following 5 minutes we talked about everything but my audition.

In spite of the obvious, for the next two days, I was depressed and felt like a failure for not being able to 'nail' the part. None of my own savvy advice could console me and I was ready to tear up all of my union cards.

It took the wisdom of my neighbor to set me straight. She asked me if I had gotten the part and I told her my story. Well, she laughed so hard she almost doubled up. "Butchy! You're closer to an ax murderer than 'butchy!" I gave that girl a great big hug, she'd just made my day. She was right. I could have been Dame Edith Evans and I wouldn't have gotten that part.

- **Each day is a dress rehearsal for the role we are eventually to play.**
- **In all circumstances be the best you can be, that is what really matters.**
- **Sometimes all it takes is an outside voice of reason to help us clearly see.**
- **If one dream dies, there is always another right behind it.**

What Was I Thinking

My mother is always as close as my next thought.

A Mother's Nudge

There isn't a day that goes by that I wish I could pick up the phone and talk to Mother. While I never used to admit it, she did really know what was best for me. I now know her love for my brother and myself had no boundaries and although she was the first to see that *her* needs were met, she was selfless when it came to her children.

It is with deep regret that only after her passing at age 92 that I have become so wise about my mother's loyalty. Sometimes I would fight her intuition into the ground, but when I *did* listen to her she usually was right.

Case in point. "Sandra, there is a perfect job I heard about for you today. A teacher's position on television." Mother had read about a children's program that was auditioning in Baltimore near my university.

"Are you crazy?" I argued. "I don't have any qualifications to do that. I don't even have a teaching degree." But as usual, Mother's persistence wore me down and I went to the audition.

I am ashamed to admit she was right and it changed the course of my life. Against all odds, on a dark rainy day, I got the job. All due to my mother's overwhelming faith in me.

"I always knew you could do it," she said. The children's program was *Romper Room.* This one job gave me the beginning of a wonderful career in television.

The other day a friend of mine was chasing her empty garbage cans rolling in the wind away from her house.

"As I ran, my 70 year-old heart was marching like a brass band trying to catch up to the parade and I could hear my mother say, 'Run faster Betty, you can catch them.' It's amazing, but after all these years, my mother has never left my side," she added.

A mother's influence in her child's life, whether positive or negative, lasts a lifetime. Perhaps small remnants are worn away with time, but the fabric they have woven into our lives is there forever.

I consider myself one of the children in this world to have been blessed with the nurturing of a mother who was, most of the time, able to get it right.

What Was I Thinking

What's In Your Jeans?

Spring is here and summer will be in full bloom before we can hide the donut box. Out come the exercise outfits, weights and walking shoes. Not much time to loose those extra pounds that have mysteriously appeared around your middle.

Hit the gym for six days a week and you think you've found a disciplined fix for your winter transgressions. I don't know about you, but not being a person who likes routine, this really does seem overwhelming and honestly makes me a little tired, just thinking about it.

Well, if you need a reprieve from your routine, take it outside! You can exercise when and where you want and it won't empty your wallet. But it will tighten up your abs, thighs and legs! Just looking at my 40-year-old daughter who got me started on my 'hill routine' is proof that it does work!

What Was I Thinking

I love to walk. Sometimes alone. By myself I can gather a good pace and keep it there. I vary the walk and do the hills one day, combination the next and sometimes just flat out do the level terrain.

In the winter I have the lengthy Miami beach, but at my home in New Jersey there is a small state park on the flat walk and I stop and do what is called an abdominal kick out. (I'm at the comfortable age where I could care less who is watching). I first read about this move developed by personal trainer, Nancy Cole and thought I would try it. It's great and now I incorporate in in my weekly walks.

Just sit on the edge of the bench with your hands behind your hips and fingers pointed toward your back. Lean back slightly, squeeze your abs and draw your knees in toward your chest. With our toes pointed, deliberately extend your legs straight out and up. Then, draw your knees back in toward your chest. Next, extend your legs toward the ground and back again toward your chest. Try two sets of 15 to 20 repetitions.

I find training outdoors not only gives me a change of atmosphere, but it is double duty to chase away depression. See if you can fit some outdoor exercise activity into your day. The variety could help you stay motivated.

Out, Out Damn Wrinkle

No. Even if you are over 40. This is not about skin care. Although wrinkles and lines are a favorite subject of mine and how to avoid them, I'm talking here about packing.

Years ago I learned from Rosemary Clooney how to roll my casual clothes and to layer with tissue paper or plastic cleaning bags my finer clothes. When she was on the road, she had to learn to pack without the need of an iron. So if you want to pack without having to look like a bag-lady at your destination of choice. Here are the basics to consider, please read on.

- **Roll T-shirts, shorts, micro fiber clothes.**

- Consider the size of your suitcase/ full not stuffed.
- Lay out clothes and then pick size of suitcase. Consider carry weight as well.
- Place shirts on the bottom, then dresses, then pants.
- Stack tops, unfolded by placing wrinkle-prone tops toward the bottom of a pile and less easily wrinkled ones toward the top.
- Fold the shirts in half from the bottom. You now have a rectangular bundle of shirts, place it in your suitcase.
- Drape long dressed in the suitcase so that the ends hang over the sides.
- Place pants, and skirts on a flat surface, fold each in half lengthwise. Stack pants and shirts on top of one another. Fold the stack over, so that its length is halved.
- Place your stack of items on top of the dresses, then fold the ends of the dresses over the pants and skirts.

If you are flying don't forget to pack essential items, including medications, jewelry, electronics and basic toiletries.

News Junky

The other day I asked my son, who is in the very stressful music business, what I should tell people to help them reduce their stress. His reply was, "Tell them stop watching or reading the news."

Now that's cheeky advice, I thought knowing how I, a news junky, personally react to everything that is going on in the world from war to kidnapping, murder and child abuse. Of course, a forever withdraw from the worst in the world is not practical, but it sure wouldn't hurt for a few days or even a week. Wasn't it Depok Chopra who said the same thing?

The peace of mind I would have not being

bombarded with negative and horrific news about the transgressions of the human race every waking moment of my day would be refreshing. And I think I would go one step further than my son's advice and 'x' Reality TV.

My husband loves The Contender and my mother's heart races with anxiety when I see these young fighters pulverizing one another in front of their young children and the world. What is to become of us!

Most of us are sponges and can't help but absorb negative energy when we feel the stress of a world that seems to have gone wrong. I think tomorrow, I'm going to take my son's advice and see how I feel in a few days. Come along with me to the land of television-free!

Lessons I've Learned From My Pups

While walking along the beach with my rescued pups, Harley, a Shih Tzu, and a Chihuahua Skipper that my daughter in Lexington, Kentucky found in a shelter for me, I was thinking about life and as individuals how our perception on "just being" varies.

Harley merrily bounces along in life without a care, along the beach, in the park, everywhere. People just love him because in spite of his bow-legs, pigeon-toes and under-bite, Harley is a clown, loving me, I think, but loyal to no one but himself. I often fear that should I forget to be a good mom, he would easily take up with another who's pastures seem greener. Harley's cheerful independence is catching and it makes me happy to be with him

Skipper, on the other hand, is like Crazy Glue, I can't walk, talk, sit or work without his trying to get on my lap, under my feet or stuck to my side. I can't pick him up without his trying to infect me with every germ he has breeding in his long and slimy tongue. I try to give Skipper the extra love he needs, but his neediness and blatant insecurity sometimes makes me weary. In other words, I do love him in spite of himself, but Skipper sometimes weighs me down at times.

Harley's Lesson · We each are unique packages, not one like another. It is our inner package that shines through with independence and a zest for life that helps make us attractive to others. Having confidence in that difference and realizing that it does truly make us special allows us the freedom to be happy with ourselves and honors the fact that we are comfortable with who we are.

Skipper's Lesson · Clinging vines belong on wallpaper. Few things are more self destructive than thinking that your happiness depends upon another person, career goal or material object. This behavior invariably produces a "Is that all there is?" emptiness at the end of the rainbow. Realizing that your acceptance of and belief in yourself is primary to how you are perceived by others. You are special and celebrate that!

Finding Your Sanctuary

Your home can be just that place. Where when you close the door behind you, stress is left outside and your soul is nurtured inside. No matter how chaotic things are at home, with a few simple steps you can create a more comfortable environment around you.

- Bring the outdoors in; green plants, cut flowers, blooming bulbs, as well as pieces of wood, rocks and other natural elements. These can bring a feeling of nature indoors.
- Surround your senses with beauty. Artwork, fragrance, smooth textures and calming sounds all provide a pleasant environment in which to relax.
- Clean out clutter. A low-maintenance home is refreshing after a hectic day of work, errands and chores. Fewer items can mean less frustration.

What Was I Thinking

My Place In the Queue

Most of us look forward to the holidays and sharing good times with family and friends. It is also a time when we reflect on the year just ending and the new year quickly approaching. It is a time for reflection and correction. At least that is how I look at it.

I have always tried to instill in my children a good work ethic by being their best example. But the older I get, the more I have come to realize that although hard work and dedication are admirable qualities, you need something else.

The magic ingredient is faith, but not just in yourself. It's the belief that your life has a purpose even if you don't know it yet.

This is a recognition that you belong on this planet at this time in history. That's all you need. If you lose sight of this belonging, just listen to the beat of your heart; it's the metronome of existence that marks your time on Earth.

What Was I Thinking

Symphony

On a wintry day I tilted my head to catch a snowflake on my tongue. I felt nothing.

No taste. No cold.

Alone it was lost.

I bent and cupped the snow in my bare hand. I felt the cold.

In magnitude its Soul came to life.

I could see their brilliance.

What Was I Thinking

Me. Me, Me

Writing is a never-ending challenge and especially writing about oneself. I find it much harder than creating characters from one's imagination.

With her imagination a writer can control the character and the twist and turns of the character's life within the story and back-story you have created for her.

As we go about our business on this planet, unfortunately, as we all know, we have little control of our own story. They say life is sometimes stranger than fiction, and that is what makes it often too hard to put on paper.

On the other hand, reading stories about people's lives often helps us with our own life. Sometimes we feel isolated within our pain and problems and our joys.

Knowing we share a common bond of universal trials in life with others while we are here, sometimes, makes it easier to identify, knowing we are not aliens walking alone.

Circle Of Light

Time went by too quickly for us I thought, as I was sorting and putting the vestiges of her life with us in boxes. A few for Goodwill, others containing cherished mememtos to de distributed to family members wishing just a small part of her life.

How outraged she would be seeing her life so neatly bundled, compartmentalized for equal distribution. Mother was always a free spirit and loved to race with the winds at her back. She never stopped experiencing and it was only after she drove through a stop sign when she was eighty-seven and hurt her neck that her wings had to be clipped. She had to give up her work as a top telemarketer for an executive publication. Regardless of her age, few were strong enough to say 'no' to mother's eagerness. I know I never could.

There was a time, as a young woman, I got caught up in my own life and found myself too busy writing my own script. I only considered my mother a bit player in my drama. I now know she was the star...not me. It was her unselfish light that shined the brightest and guided me along my way.

My mother may be gone and I will always miss her, but the circle never closes. I am a mother and a grandmother now and Mother's light continues to shine through me to my children and through them to their children. Her circle of light lives on through us.

Raga Or Rap

There have been so many love songs written that if I had a penny for every one, I wouldn't have to buy lottery tickets.. Music has always been good for matters of the heart, but now a new study shows that listening to music really has a heart-healing effect.

Listening to music that has a slow or meditative tempo has a relaxing effect on people, slowing their breathing and heart rate, whereas listening to faster music with a more upbeat tempo has the opposite effect - speeding up respiration and heart rate. Research shows that there is a potential stress-reducing health benefit of music.

The style of the music or an individual's music

preference seems less important than the tempo of the music. The present study suggests that the appropriate selection of music, alternating fast and slower rhythms interspersed with paused can be used to induce relaxation and may, therefore, be beneficial in heart disease and stroke.

One of the best gifts I have ever received is an iPod on which I have downloaded hours of music. This little gizmo that is no bigger than half of an Almond Joy bar has saved my sanity many of days.

I just disconnect the outside world with the tiny earpieces and enter into my own utopia until calm returns to my immediate world.

Color Me Stressless

The first time I hosted Romper Room my knees were shaking so rapidly, I thought I would collapse. The opening night of my first leading role in an off-Broadway play I was terrified I would forget my lines halfway through. None of these dire predictions happened and I have gone on and done numerous performances and spoken in front of audiences comfortably.

Unfortunately my earlier naiveté in how to channel my stress and anxiety did not allow me go without stress in life.

Little things would always bother me, but it was not

until I realized that unless it was a 'life or death" situation I could let it go, that I was able to lessen my stress level. .

Stress can be linked to both external and internal factors, though it is the internal-or the way we react to external situations-that actually causes the stress

Unfortunately my earlier naiveté in how to channel my stress and anxiety did not allow me go without stress in life.

Little things would always bother me, but it was not until I realized that unless it was a 'life or death" situation I could let it go, that I was able to lessen my stress level.

Although I do remember an interview with the great Sir Laurence Oliver who admitted that he threw up before every performance and could not shake his initial stage fright. So I do put myself in good company in the uncontrollable stress arena. But I now know stress can be controlled by thoughts. Meditation and letting go are the best two tools we have to lessen our anxiety and stress as we go about out daily lives.

Living A Life Of Purpose

Purpose serves as a principle around which we organize our lives. And as Richard Leider once noted, "The purpose of life is to live a life of purpose."

During my career as a news anchor and talk show host, I found that the most successful persons in their fields that had reached the pinnacle of success had a drive and definite purpose from early childhood. Those that were climbing the ladder of success who had no direct purpose or lacked humility proved not to go very far in spite of their prospect for great success.

Henry Miller once said, "that to be purpose-driven you must develop an interest in life as you see it. The people, things, literature, music-the world is so rich, simply throbbing with rich treasures, beautiful souls, interesting people.

Forget yourself and it will happen.

Feng Shui Me

When we moved into our South Beach house a friend helped me rearrange furniture and hang mirrors. When I opened the door for him, he practically had a heart attack. Apparently my theory to place mirrors on a dark wall so they reflect light was a pure "no-no" in the world of Feng Shui. My luck was going right out the door every time it was opened and the outside light reflected off my antique mirror.

He immediately set me straight like a good Feng Shui Santa Clause and together we went about giving our home the right space clearing and purifying rituals. In the old days these rituals were usually undertaken by Taoist or Buddhist monks who chanted special prayers accompanied by the clashing of cymbals and beating gongs as well as the burning of incense.

Luckily after the space and furniture was organized for the best Feng Shui, I happened to already have a gong from Pier 1 and incense that I dug from a bottom drawer that came all the way from the New Jersey shore hopelessly forgotten under my linens. Breathing a sigh of relief, Charles Feng Shui-ed our house and I knew we were going to be okay when it was over. He saved the day and our house surely was blessed. No thanks to my Feng Shui ignorance.

I Remember Mama

So many of us at some point in our lives have tried to juggle six balls in the air without dropping them while holding the car keys in our teeth and a bag of groceries in our arms while listening to our cell phone ringing hopelessly somewhere unknown to us. It is at these impossible moments that I think my mother.

My mother was always there for me. In spite of what she had going on in her life, she never refused to listen to what I thought were the awful trials in mine. She was my strongest cheerleader throughout my life with her and I miss her strong and positive shoulder many days when I need a hug and an affirming push.

Remember was my mother's insistence that I audition for Romper Room when I thought it was hopeless to do so. It was her undying faith in my talent and ability that let me go to New York from Ohio to follow my dreams.

I once was told that a mother's job was not to make leaning necessary, but to make letting go easy. She did just that.

Mother knew when to let go and allow me to use my wings to fly.

So on those impossible days when everything seems to go wrong I remember that her faith in a better tomorrow never proved wrong.

Healthy Selfishness

Recently, I find myself less willing and sometimes overwhelmed with responsibilities to others that I always assumed was my duty. In the past that is the dynamic that I have put forth.

I thought I would share with you my thoughts from a different perspective about the new seeds that are springing fresh life into the old landscape of our attitudes and relationships.

Selfishness has always been a negative word for me. It was only recently that the world received the good news that a degree of it is not only okay, but an important ingredient in living a full life and its presence-or lack of it-can make a difference in both the big and small issues in your life.

The true cost of self-denial is high. In failing to put our own needs first, we hope or assume others will give to us as we give to them. But they don't always. And an unhealthy dynamic begins.

Many see healthy selfishness as a higher level of mental function that can help you reach your full potential. People who practice healthy selfishness have a zest for living, a joy that comes from savoring one's accomplishments.

Healthy selfishness opens the door to a life of freedom-freedom from being ruled by the opinions and demands of others as well as freedom from the voices in your own mind, often left over from childhood.

Healthy selfishness involves accepting your weaknesses and imperfections without beating yourself up. It means nurturing yourself and loving yourself unconditionally.

Put yourself in control. Here are your options:

- **Small steps.** (i.e.) Don't offer your significant other the television remote right away when beginning an evening of television together.
- **Longer Strides.** (i.e.) Don't offer your significant other the television remote.
- **Life-changing leaps.** (i.e.) Hide the remote in a safe place and then hold it securely in your hand and control it all evening.

Heavenly Sign Language

"She's gone," the doctor on the other end of the phone said quietly, "She passed away in her sleep this morning."

And so, the moment that we knew was near, but were never really ready for had finally come. Quiche Lorraine, our beloved waggle-tailed, shaggy friend had grown weary in her almost twentieth year and crossed over the Rainbow Bridge without us.

As we gathered under the shadow of the little blue spruce we had planted to celebrate the birth of our first grandchild, we bid farewell to our pal and wondered at the mystery of life, hoping there was a place in God's heaven for all of His creatures.

We each said a prayer while sanding where the earth covered our friend and asked that we should have her tolerance of our faults, her cheerfulness when asked to serve, her trust that we would not fail her, and most of all, her unconditional love for us that never wavered in her years as our loyal friend.

There was silence as we each struggled with our loss, when my little grandchild's voice broke the stillness, "Remember, Nana, what Mommy said? If you have a question, just ask God for a sign? Can we ask for a sign?"

The following day I received another call, this time it was from my daughter. "You know, Mother, as I was walking and admiring the beautiful blue sky I looked in the clouds, and she was there. In the center of the blue I saw Quiche, white and fluffy, her ears flying and her tail all feathered, you remember how she used to jump when she was young? She was jumping. It was our sign, the one we asked for telling us that she was okay."

I have no doubt that when I am ready to cross over the Rainbow Bridge that all of the people in my life that I have loved will be there to greet me, and maybe, just maybe, my loyal friend, Quiche, will be there on the other side just beyond the bend jumping and wagging her feathered tail, waiting for me.

Through My Daughter's Eyes

When I was a child an older cousin who had become a doctor walked with me along the beach and explained to me that God was everywhere; in the waves that lapped the shore; in the seashells and even in the grains of sand beneath my feet.

As I felt the minute grains sift between my toes as

we walked, I tried to imagine a big person like God squeezing into such a small place. Wondering if my cousin was teasing me, "Is he in trees, birds and snakes?" I challenged.

He assured me that I could find God in all things. And so began my quest to find my cousin's God. Somehow I just couldn't see God as a frog.

The years went by and I never told anyone about my conversation with my cousin. I tucked it away somewhere secret within me.

"Take a deep breath," my husband told me as he held my hand.

Just when I didn't think I could take it anymore, I pushed and suddenly a marvelous sound echoed in the delivery room, bouncing off the sterile walls in sharp staccato notes. The music of a new life.

My baby was placed in my arms and I looked at her funny little face. As I felt her warmth against my body, the conversation with my cousin so many years ago came back to me. I finally got what he was trying to say.

My God is Life, here and now, and through my daughter's eyes I will see Him in the trees, in the waves, and maybe even in a slippery old frog.

Growing Wings

Little did I know when I gave birth to my third child, a bouncing boy with the lung power of a trumpeting elephant, that it would be of interest to the music world that my rock star son was indeed born on July 21, just hours after the United States made history with the first moon landing.

Had I known his birthday would be an occasion others might be interested in, perhaps I would had paid more attention to that day. Anyone who has given birth knows just getting though the process is enough. Having a child land on earth while the astronauts were walking on the moon was not exactly on my mind as I headed out to work that morning on Romper Room. My labor pains started in route and I barely made it to the hospital in time.

While I was raising my children, I loved them all for each of the special wonders they brought to my life. But back then, just getting them dressed with matching socks, fed and off to school without losing one of them, as I ran out the door to work was just about all I could manage. Far away in a distant time were my dreams of a life on the stage. My stage was my children's life.

I have come to accept that my plan for my life was not as important as the one already mapped out for me - giving my children wings.

Besides, you can't beat the perks. Free rock t-shirts and the privilege of letting the band crash at your house when passing through.

It's Never Too Late

Several years ago during a discussion with a successful businessman, he confided to me that the most valuable advice he has ever gotten was from a mentor he had early in his career, "Don't be so obsessed with your life's plan, because there is God's plan. In the long run, Son, your plan doesn't matter."

Since that conversation, I have thought about how this advice could relate, in general, within each segment of our lives.

While walking though our local mall the other day, I caught the tail end of a conversation between two teen-aged boys.

"…you can't help it man, s--t happens."

And as much as I disliked the vernacular, the message was there. Things do happen to us beyond our control, but we don't have to become a victim because our life doesn't seem to be going as planned.

Life throws us all kind of weird and unexpected stuff, it just does. But the answer is how we work through it. We do have choices and, those choices have consequences.

If we work hard through a situation, while at the same time, positively focusing on each day, one at a time, and quit trying to control the direction of the outcome, wonderful things can begin to happen.

The most important footnote on this thought is that it is never too late to begin letting it happen in your life.

"I am putty at the mercy of my own hands"

Reinventing Myself

For several months before I started writing this, I had found myself fascinated with magazine and television features focusing on the traumas women in America face as they hit forty and beyond.

Each of these informative pieces warned me to keep a stiff upper lip because they are not as plump as they used to be; instructed me to try not to feel rejected when the construction workers no longer ogle my drooping behind. It will either get wider or soon disappear all together depending on my body type.

Articles reminded me to not take it personally when my young grandchild kisses me on the cheek and remarks the henna in my hair smells funny. And to please try not to have a breakdown when I look in the mirror and see my mother's face looking back at me.

Since I could not ignore that I had experienced all of these traumas, what was I left to think? Aging is a natural process and there is nothing I can do about it short of major surgery, so get over it. Unless I was willing to spend 10 hours a week at the gym, ditch the car and jog for groceries, and accept that the new Mercedes my hairdresser drives should have my name on it.

All of this angst just to fight for my place in society and to be accepted as anything but and over-the-hill reject?

I am a survivor I kept telling myself, but knew I was in trouble when after stepping on the scale one morning and discovering I had gained seven pounds for no reason whatsoever, I began coveting that last Krispy Kreme my husband had left in the box for later. With my saliva glands in overdrive and as my hand slipped into foreign territory within the green and red box to make contact with that sticky delight, I knew I had finally gone over the edge.

Then to add the final cruel blow. One that has sent

me running to my computer in protest, was a television show featuring a dermatologist instructing us aging females not to despair for there was painless cosmetic hope to keep us looking better longer.

She began to through the age groups..30's…40's..

I managed to find a pen swallowed up beneath my husband's mountain of morning clutter and was eagerly awaiting her advice for me; a desperate woman who was game to try almost anything short of swimming the English Channel to stay in shape and hang on to whatever va-va-voom I could.

Well, my anticipation was short lived. It seems that if you are over 60 there were no 60's helpful hints. All hope stopped at the 50's according to this segment.

Moving to Europe where a woman my age might not be viewed as past her prime, was out of the question. How on earth could my family survive without me-the woman who had "Caregiver" tattooed on her forehead.

Right there and then, I vowed to reinvent myself from the inside out and try to be the best of who I was right now. I would explore uncharted territories, suppressed treasures, searching to discover places within myself I had not dared discover. Places where as a younger woman, I was too intimidated to let blossom.

Already I have begun to take control and change my life each day by doing instead of dreaming and by doing, proving that it is never too late.

My reflection to the world around me is younger, more honest and more alive because of not only how I perceive myself, but how I allow myself to be perceived.

Although I am not ready to give up the 'window dressing' that makes me feel better when I look in the mirror, the inward richness I am discovering is more meaningful and is turning out to be more refreshing than the ultimate haircut, facial or massage. I'm on my way with winded wings through this Great Beauty Mirage and I intend to enjoy every minute of my flight.

And I have to admit a wolf whistle here and there is a great tail wind. Even if it is coming from an old gray fox with a cane.

(Shortly after I wrote this piece I was asked by the NBC's Later Today Show to be featured on an about-town-beauty bargain feature. The following week the segment aired and the dialogue began..."Sandra Hart, actress and retired grandma..." So there it was, misinformation for all the world to hear. Sure I am an actress. Sure I am a grandmother. But I am not at all retired. The bottom line is: all the surface beautifying didn't matter. I was still locked in the 'aging box', doomed to knock and cry forever, *"Excuse me...Excuse me...let me out'ta here!"*

Guest Angst In Los Angeles

The bottom line is that men are clueless. We women know that the expensive, fluffy and decorative guest towels that match the well-planned décor of the only bathroom the guests are allowed to experience, are never, never to be used.

I am quite an esthetic fanatic myself, but not exactly for guest bathroom towels. My guests are welcome to luxuriate in the pleasant setting I have prepared just for them.

What Was I Thinking

Recently we stopped in Los Angeles to visit with a male friend of my husband's whose wife has decorated their home in museum-quality style. Now I really love this woman. She is kind and intelligent and very generous with her time in helping others. But when it comes to her house, she becomes a different sort all together.

So it was no surprise as we all showered that evening to go out when I heard a scream that rang from her cathedral ceilings and back again as she ran down the hall.

"What! How could he! Arthur is using the guest bathroom!? Nobody uses the guest bathroom!"

As I opened the door, draped in an ordinary towel I found in the under-guest-guest bathroom, I saw my husband standing there like a sheep-faced child, caught in a dastardly deed.

Our hostess quickly went into the coveted-never-used guest bathroom and proceeded to wipe the faucets spotless and clean up the chaos my husband made of her perfect-to-look-at room.

I learned a valuable lesson on our trip. How to be a more forgiving hostess, for one. And better yet, how to be a more compassionate wife. When I came home I threw out all of our old ratty towels with strings fraying at the ends and bought big fluffy premiere guest towels for Arthur.

Who cares if our bathroom floor becomes the Nile River when he showers, or if I slip into the commode in the middle of the night because he forgets to put down the lid.

Now, instead of having a post-menopausal fit if I can't find the new ten dollar herbal soap I just put at the basin, I forgivingly retrieve it in the shower from a cache of soap he constantly steals, because he forgets what he did yesterday.

I have even learned not to straighten up and fluff the couch pillows each time a guest has rearranged them.

I leave my grandchild's handprints for a bit longer than usual on my mirrors. And now and then, when I am really feeling frisky, I tilt a candle in the candelabra just a bit to remind myself life isn't perfect and human feeling and comfort are worth more than material things with esthetic balance.

What Was I Thinking

" Now faith is the assurance of things hoped for, the conviction of things not seen." Hebrews 11:1

Dare To Do It

I believe that there is a Higher Power or external/internal entity somewhere guiding us in our daily lives. We don't have to put a name to it, that is a personal choice, but most believe there is some power bigger than us orchestrating the universe.

Yesterday while having breakfast with my daughter we talked about stepping out of one's comfort zone to get to that top of the mountain we are so afraid to climb. Dare to do it. Keep pursuing and keep believing. It doesn't take any more effort to take risks than it takes to develop a negative and defeated attitude.

In spite of the obstacles thrown into my path, I rarely doubted that my dreams would come to pass. I rarely doubted that good things were in store for me. It was only on those few occasions when I let negative doubts affect my real thoughts and actions, did I suffer.

A positive attitude doesn't come easy when thing seem to be going wrong. Unfortunately, as the Staples commercials would have you believe...there is no EASY BUTTON to fix our lives.

People who see their dreams come to pass are people who have strong resolve, some backbone: people who refuse to settle somewhere along the road.

You need to simply focus on your goal, set your course, and have the attitude, *I'm not going to settle for a little, or a bit or a small piece of happiness or success. I'm going to start living my best life now*!

"If it is well with your belly, chest and feet, the wealth of kings can give you nothing more" Horace

Feet First

If you were feeling unwell 5000 years ago in Egypt, you might well have asked to have your feet massaged. Aside from the obvious pleasure of a foot massage on the banks of the Nile, such a treatment seems to have been used for restoring the body to health.

Although it has garnered plenty of publicity of late, reflexology has a long and distinguished history. A beautiful relief in an Egyptian tomb from around

2500-2300BC. shows two men at a royal palace practicing what appears to be reflexology on the feet and hands.

In ancient China the feet were treated to stimulate the whole body. Similar treatments were common in India and Indonesia, while native Americans believed that we were connected to the earth's energies through our feet.

In recent years numerous ancient therapies have been rediscovered as interest in homeopathy, acupuncture and osteopathy, reflexology has rapidly gained a large following. Reflexology's aim is to help the body to heal itself.

A central tenet of reflexology is that illness or stress causes deposits to build up in the feet. which are not cleared away by circulation. Problems in the body are accompanied by grains and crystals in the part of the foot that represents the area. When pressure is applied by hand to these parts of the feet and the deposits are messaged away, the related part of the body will be stimulated and encouraged to heal itself.

Some doctors are starting to suggest it as complementary treatment, and hospitals are making use of it, too. It seems that this ancient treatment has passed the test of time. Our neglected feet now seem to hold the key to our whole well-being.

"Romper, Bomper, Stomper ......"

Romper Room

It seems as though in the last few years all those terribly terrific children who grew up with us on Romper Room are now ruling the world and moving and shaking in all-important circles of life.

Those who grew up in the 60's, 70's and 80's are today's power brokers of influence. The are now the bankers, brokers, directors. writers, rock stars and

CEO's of corporations. But they all have the Big Question for me when I am lucky enough to meet one of them. "Why didn't you say my name in your Magic Mirror?"

When the January 23, 1997 issue of Rolling Stone revealed to the world that my son, Emerson Hart, lead vocalist and songwriter of the band Tonic, had a mother who was the Romper Room lady, I could no longer hide in anonymity. I was dragged from underneath the rock I had been hiding since the 70's. Since then I have been forced to account for my sins.

Some of these wonderful men and women I have met at my son's concerts, either thank me, or admonish me for not saying their name in my Magic Mirror. When I explain to them that I tried my very best to name each and every one I could in the short time allotted at the end of the show to 'see' all of my Do Bees, but because of the volumes of mail I received each day, I couldn't acknowledge as many as I would have liked, they pretend to understand, but they are still not satisfied. So if you are reading this and I didn't say your name, *please* forgive me.

'Romper Bomper, Stomper Boo. Tell me, tell me true. Magic Mirror, tell me today did all my friends have fun at play? I see Michelle and John and Bill and...oh, there you are. I've been looking for you all these years. I see YOU!"

Leave It To Beaver

I have long learned to cast away the guilt of not being able to have given my children their fantasy 'Leave It To Beaver' childhood.

I have since spoken to other parents, whose children refuse to take accountability for what they perceive as mistakes in their own lives by trying to thrust the blame for their choices back to their parents. All one has to do on a daily basis is to pick up any newspaper and the same theme is shouted from its pages. 'Who me?'. 'It's not my fault!'. 'I didn't do it!.'

Outside the world of old-time television, I don't

believe there is such a being as a perfect parent or perfect child, but I do believe in accountability. I know my parents weren't perfect, but I have never blamed them for decisions I have made in my life that were less than intelligent. But somehow offspring today find it an easy escape route for facing the consequences of their decisions.

I will forever give my children my unconditional love, support and, if necessary, a cave to howl in on those 'full moon days'. But I have learned to help them take responsibility for the consequences of their adult decisions, by refusing to be a receptacle of blame for their mistakes.

I have done my best to give them wings and it is up to them to choose their own flight patterns and to be responsible for their own destinations.

Years from now, as I sit in my rocking chair at the nursing home where my dear children have placed me, I wonder what my grandchildren will be telling their old Nana about my children's parenting skills?

I don't think I will be surprised. Perfect parenting does not exist on this planet in any child's eyes and only too soon the circle comes around.

Falling In Love With Gary Cooper

As a child I always fantasized my destiny would be to fall in love with Gary Cooper and to spend my days as part of the life I saw in the movies. I thought my future held something special and believed in that dream.

Well, I have had sort of a divine life, but my childhood dreams took a back seat for awhile to what my life really was to be; nursing stitches from play injuries; spills from horses; scary rescues from Godzilla waves at the beach; tea with Barbie and her friends and ten thousand cookies baked in the middle of the night.

As a young mother, I did manage to achieve certain envious career plateaus, but not without a price. Along the way, the cost of my dreams were affecting my children.

I was missing basketball games, school plays and Brownie meetings. Basically, I was missing their lives.

I had walked away from the gift I had given them in order to chase my own windmills. I thought I could have it all.

That is until the day I drove by a school bus stop on my way to work and saw a mother wiping away her child's tears, an feeling my own well up inside of me. I knew it was time to wake up. I had to get off my carousel and pass the brass ring to another.

On my youngest child's third birthday, I gave up a promising career, walked away from my life's dream and began to enjoy the wonder of those three unique beings chosen to walk with me on this journey.

My colleagues and others close to me questioned my sanity, but I knew it was the right decision for me. I have never looked back with regret. It has proved to be better than going to Disneyland.

A Lesson in Caring

It was the kind of evening when the wind found every opening in my heavy winter wrappings. There was no escaping the chill that went through my bones as I sat on the stern deck of the Queen Elizabeth as we sailed down the Hudson toward the Atlantic and the beginning of our 109 day world cruise.

With my beret pulled down over my ears and scarf wrapped around my neck as high as possible, I leaned against the railing facing the winds watching the magnificent New York night skyline seeming so close swim slowly past.

Weeks before my friends Lou and Cathy who live

in the East Village vowed that they would add to our send-off by signaling to us from the end of Christopher Street pier as we sailed by. It seemed a great idea at the time, until our sailing was delayed into the darkness and severe winter weather moved in. So much for a personal send-off, I disappointedly thought, Lou would be working and Cathy would be alone.

As we moved along, suddenly I saw a flicker...a blinking beam of bright light coming from the Christopher Street pier. Once, twice, three times. She had come. She had come in the darkness, and waited in the cold to wish us a bon voyage as she had promised.

Think Before You Speak

I used to be so conscious of 'doing the right thing'. Afraid not to follow protocol by putting others needs and wants before mine.   It took dinner with a president to set me straight.

In 1980 my husband and I hosted a financial seminar at the Greenbrier, the famous West Virginia resort within the rolling hills of that beautiful state. Not only is the Greenbrier famous for its elegance, exquisite accommodations and cuisine, but built in the bowels of this grand hotel was a secret bunker for emergency cold wartime use..

While dining with President Ford on the last

evening of our conference we spoke of things politic and personal. President Ford was handsome, charming and quite knowledgeable on world affairs and the current state of our union. He was so charming and interesting that I began to think of him as I would a nice next door neighbor and almost forgot his credentials and powerful position.

The Secret Service who had been hovering in the background began to nervously look at their watches and finally came and whispered in my ear that the president had his plane waiting for him and it was time for him to leave.

Having the 'obey' antennas well extended, I turned to President Ford and politely relayed the Secret Service's message.

He turned and snapped in a voice of complete power, "I am the President and I haven't had my desert yet!"

Memories Never Die

Several years ago I had just completed a successful reading of my one-woman show about my life with my husband. My son was finishing his first record album and invited me to come to Los Angles to hear some of his new music, including a song about his father.

When I arrived at the recording studio, a facility that could have served easily as a small luxury hotel, my son buzzed me in. I met the producer and got a tour of rooms with gigantic mixing boards and as long as the runway at JFK. But unfortunately my mission to hear my son's new song was impossible because of the production schedule. I came home, instead, with a tape of the song.

What Was I Thinking

I put my son's tape on a back shelf in my mind, until one early spring day. I was cleaning out my attic that was groaning from twenty-five years of loving neglect. As I was working my way through the boxes, my life with my family passed before my eyes; the old Brownie movie projector; my daughter's hairless Tiny Tears doll; my son's bedraggled one-eyed Snoopy; a box of my son's music tapes he had recorded five years before his move to Los Angeles. It was all there, evidence of a life gone by, patiently waiting for a new life again.

That evening I opened the dusty box and looking through the tapes, I remembered the new one my son had given to me two weeks prior, and popped it into the recorder.

The soft sounds of his acoustic guitar opened up to a full, rich sound, setting the stage for his voice and lyrics; his story; his pain.

That night was as though I was listening to his music for the first time with new clarity. As I listened, old wounds of my own that I thought were healed, split open to the fleshy part of my soul and I wept for our pain. Once again my children's entwined with mine.

Our dreams; our anger, our loss. It was all there. His words were saying it for all of us. Memories never die.

"One is the loneliest number that you'll ever do." **John Farnham**

One Is The Loneliest Number ?

Come on, John. The number one doesn't always get a fair shake. So many songs including the one with the famous line in our above title. 'One' means heartache, single, loneliness, by myself and all of the other negative images they want us to conjure up about poor little "1".

I really am hankerin' to change the image of that single diget. Isn't 'one' the primary, the very first number in our numeric system? Without '1' there would be no starting. And with all of the other infinite numbers trailing behind, it certainly is not

121

lonely. How about " a bird in the hand is worth two in the bush"? Now, that's more like it.

If you really think about it we are never alone. We always have ourselves and if you believe, a Higher Power to call on on a 24/7 basis. That's not too shabby.

For me being by myself gives me the opportunity to do as I please, have quality time for me. How many harried young mothers I have spoken with, have resorted to locking themselves in the bathroom for a few moments just to be alone.

When you are alone and feeling sorry for yourself just think of the biggest bore you have ever met and thank your lucky stars that person is not in the room with you. Embrace your 'oneness'.

If you are lonely reach out to another and give of yourself through a friendly call, read an inspirational book, or get out and take a walk around the block and get those blues-erasing endorphins going.

And always remember tomorrow is another day and a chance to be number one again, ahead of the pack and at the top of the heap. Because if you learn to love yourself, you will be your own best company.

Vi and Ron

.

Before 911 sometimes the only ones we could turn to were friends. In 1977 I wrapped my small children in blankets and in the darkness headed my Camero toward the next town to find a safe haven. My body was shaking with fear and uncertainty as I turned into Ron and Vi's driveway.

As Ron helped us from the car the warm light behind their open door and my friend Vi"s calm presence helped ease my embarrassment and guilt having had to disturb them so late in the night. They were my friends. The knew my husband and they knew his schizophrenia. They knew our secret and with their selflessness reached out their arms to embrace and comfort us in our hour of need.

I and my children have come a long way since that frightening night, but I will forever be grateful for their kindness and friendship during that very difficult time in my life. Vi and Ron are pure examples of Michael Berg's teachings in his book, "The Secret". How fortunate I am that they are in my bag of marbles.

My Wild Pony

The other day, while leisurely reading the New York Times and getting ready to hand the Automotive Section over to my husband, my heart flipped when my eyes scanned the first section page. An old love of mine that I hadn't seen in years was staring me in the face. The aristocratic and sporty nose; the classic look that has aged so well. There in beautiful Hugger Orange was a picture of my old 1969 Chevrolet Camaro. That year Chevrolet built a short run of Camaros with aluminum-block 427 engines. Only 69 were built and I just happened to have the one designed and fitted with special spoilers by my husband's friend, Don Yenko, the famous NASCAR driver.

My car had been on the cover of *Car and Driver Magazine*. Don's father owned a Chevrolet dealership in Canonsburg, Pennsylvania, and when I saw this Hugger Orange beauty in his showroom, I had to have it. My husband had a fit, but I bought the car, anyway.

Don Yenko was one of my husband's best friends. We often socialized with Don and his wife, Faith, and attended races together. I invited Faith to be on Romper Room for Show & Tell with her daughters and their big pet rabbit and through the years we enjoyed many family celebrations together.

Now, being a part of the racing crowd was not something that I yearned to do, but I sometimes tagged along with my husband on weekends just for the after-race festivities. Besides Don had his own plane, so it was easy to get in and out of race locations easily. Don was one of those people whose persona made up for his lack of physical handsomeness. When I first met him, I couldn't believe that he was *the lothario* that I had heard so much about. But after I got to know him, I could see why women found him attractive. The outside package wasn't what it seemed. Same for the car.

The only downside of driving my car, was that while I had my Yenko Camaro, I was a definite victim of profiling. I got more tickets in that car than

I have ever had in my life. Easing through stop signs; going through yellow lights, you name it...that orange car was a red flag for ticketing.

I drove my Camaro for over ten years and finally sold it to one of my daughter's boyfriends. A week later he wrapped it around a tree. He didn't get hurt, but my dear old Camaro didn't survive. It was totaled. The powerful engine was too much for him and he lost control going around a bend in the road a bit faster than he should have. A very sad ending for my Hugger Orange love.

The irony of it is that Don also had his life prematurely snuffed out. He lost his life when the plane he was piloting crashed. His death was not only a tragic loss to his family and friends, but to the loyal Camaro and Corvette aficionados as well as the NASCAR drivers and fans.

But bringing back fond memories of old friends was certainly good closure for me. Thinking about Don and Faith and seeing my old car again, I realize how lucky I was to be able to sit in the cockpit-like atmosphere of my automobile as I went from ticket to ticket. I didn't appreciate much of that until I picked up the Times. How lucky I was to be part of the Yenko generation and an original owner of a 1969 Camaro *and* to have had one of the last rides on my very own 'G.M. Wild Pony'!

What Was I Thinking

"If I had known what my life was going to be, I would have asked for a round trip ticket."

The Carnival

When I was 16 my parents let me go to Lake Erie with my older girlfriends and two mother chaperons for a holiday. Vermillion On The Lake was a lakeside vacation community with a boardwalk amusement area within walking distance. It was there that I had my first date with a local boy who along with his friends showed us 'summer girls' around.

He bought tickets for the Ferris wheel and I hadn't the courage to tell him I suffered from motion sickness. That ride seemed never to end and I un-strapped from my seat as sick as a dog. And to make matters worse we all went for a hamburger at the local diner. Now life for me, has been at times roller coaster sending me up and down, but my first

129

date was hell as I choked down the urge to be sick and ignore the whirling sensation in my stomach the whole evening we were sitting in the diner.

Looking back I'm sure he thought I was the last person he wanted to see again, I couldn't even give him a peck on the cheek as he walked me to our cabin door.

At the time I thought it was the worst day of my life, but I have since lived through much worse and much better days. And I have to believe that there has been more to my life that matters than a carnival of events in between.

Life really is a cabaret that I want to never leave.

Impromptu Moments

As an actress I always enjoy those impromptu moments when I have to listen to my fellow actors and then react by my gut or fly by the seat of my pants emotionally and verbally. Those moments always keep a performer on her best mental edge.

Unfortunately, once off the stage, I admit my skills in real life are not that great. I always think of what I should have or could have said long after the encounter has happened.

During a recent trip to London I headed for Bond Street, with its very picturesque road winding along and creating a narrow pathway for some of the most magnificent shops in London. It is among one of my favorite streets in the world where you must walk almost touching shoulders with other shoppers along the narrow way.

While savoring visions swirling in my head of the wonderful credit card opportunities that lay ahead of me, I tried to ignore the man who had popped from an art gallery and insisted walking at my pace and getting into my 'personal space'.

Annoyed at his arrogance, I kept my eyes straight ahead and didn't even glance his way. 'What a creep', I though to myself as I finally decided to give him a less than friendly stare as I quickly crossed the street to get rid of him. Our eyes met.

Well, if there had been a manhole available, I would have dived right in. Tall, tan and gorgeous, there he was receiving my 'ugly American' scowl-the actor and self-styled celebrity, George Hamilton!

I was so embarrassed that I almost humiliated myself more by tripping as I ran across the small street to escape from my stupidity. I couldn't get away from George and Bond Street fast enough.

A few days later, wanting to satisfy my credit card addiction on Bond Street before ending my vacation and forgiving myself for being such an idiot, I returned to the scene of my crime. After visiting several stores, I stopped by the Maud Frizon window to look at the shoe display.

Suddenly I was aware of a presence behind me

checking to see what was capturing my attention. My heart almost stopped. I couldn't believe the reflection I saw in the window. It belonged to the one and only George Hamilton.

"We have to stop meeting like this" he said with his white perfect teeth glistening within his perfectly tanned smile. "Husband?"

My mind went blank, and the following events are a little hazy in my memory, but I think I do remember turning toward him and giving a slight idiotic embarrassed giggle with my "Yes."

What seemed an eternity was probably no more than a few seconds, "Too bad," he replied with a wink that crinkled the skin around his perfect eyes, and he was off to continue his journey down Bond Street and I was left to think of what I should have, could have said, or wanted to say to George Hamilton.

As Mark Twain said, "The difference between the *almost-right* word and the *right* word is really a large matter-it's the difference between lightning and the lightening."

Where were my brilliant repartee impromptu skills and the right words when I so needed them!

The moral to this story is that sometimes invasion of one's personal space is not altogether a bad thing. Especially if it is George Hamilton.

What Was I Thinking

"Like the sturdy Day Lily, true friendship has strong roots and life that returns and grows in abundance year after year. But like all things in nature, neglect it and it will surely die."

My Bag Of Marbles

Our good old friend Webster defines friendship as" a **person attached to another by feelings or personal regard."** In thinking about this article, I have tried to recall the true friendships in my life that have been able to withstand the times of change, distance and turmoil. I have eight names, exclusive of my family, that come to mind.

It was rather shocking to me that these are the only

human strings, old and new, that I could attach to my longevity kite. Over a span of 60 plus years I have gathered a small circle of those with whom I have closely shared high personal regard and feelings. Some of these I see more than others, but they are all in my personal bag of marbles. I care about them.

Feeling like a recluse and with my tail between my legs I began my research and found that I am not alone. The average person, if honest with themselves, have only a handful of lifetime relationships that have weathered change, distance and turmoil. We may have made many acquaintances in our lifetime, but few are soul mates that would be willing to sacrifice their needs for ours.

Think about it. Life has thrown us all loops. Who in your life has been and will be there unconditionally when you feel that you are about to be thrown under the bus ?

If you have such friends that are connected to defining moments in your life wouldn't it be nice to let them know you care that they are there in your bag of marbles. While you can.

Reflection

Most of us look forward to the holidays and visiting family and friends. It is also a time when we reflect on the year just ending and the new year quickly approaching.

It is a time for reflection and correction. At least that is how I look at it.

I have always tried to instill in my children a good work ethic by being their best example. But The older I get, the more I have come to realize that although hard work and dedication are admirable qualities, you need something else.

The magic ingredient is faith, but not just in

yourself.

It's the belief that your life has a purpose even if you don't know it yet. This is a recognition that you belong on this planet at this time in history. That's all you need. If you lose sight of this belonging, just listen to the beat of your heart; it's the metronome of existence our time on Earth.

Snow Flakes

On a winter's day I tilted my head to
  catch a snowflake on my tongue.

I felt nothing.

No taste. No cold.

Alone it was lost.

I bent and cupped the snow in my bare hand.

I felt the cold.

In magnitude its Soul came to life.

I could see their brilliance.

I could feel their power.

What Was I Thinking

My purse is much more of an honest me than I care for you to see.

My Mother's Purse

My mother's purse is in my closet perched on the shelf beneath my blouses. Everything is still there. Her plastic tortoise reading glasses she had fixed by wiring one stem with small piece of picture hanger wire, a fake black and white string of beads curled neatly in an old black glasses case, a crinkled baggie with her makeup and tattered powder puff, more beads, green this time, her small Timex watch with the hands stopped at 10:30 and its worn-out black band. Still there are assorted bills and letters from The 700 Club and The Reader's Digest National Sweepstakes, her check book, pen and one lonely packet of Sweet 'N Low.

Mother's worn black leather bag with its sagging handle is the most physical thing that I have to remind me of her and who she was before she died in 1995 at ninety-two. She was one of the lucky ones. She just left us one day while sitting in a chair putting on lipstick. Just like that she was gone.

It took me ten years to invade her privacy by opening her valued companion. As soon as the latch was unsnapped I felt her presence. As I eavesdropped the personal contents within she was there. All of the little daily things in her life's routine that reminded me of her were there.

Somehow there was closure for me as I carefully examined Mother's final treasure chest. The material things that ruled her simple world those last days in the nursing home that were important to her were in that little black bag.

Each morning when I open my closet memories of my mother are there waiting patiently on the shelf beneath my blouses. And I wonder at life and all of the possessions surrounding me. And am made curious that perhaps my life will in the end be chronicled by what is in my purse.

The Other Side of the Cushion

I always knew when company was coming. It was the ritual Mother exercised every time someone she was trying to impress was soon to arrive at our house that gave her away. She started flipping all of the cushions on our living room furniture.

There was always one clean side reserved for company. The rest of the time the used and faded cushions were a part of our daily lives. Heaven forbid if we accidentally forgot to re-flip the cushions before we sat on them again.

I guess if plastic covers had been invented back then, Mother would have been their best advocate.

But even so, I'm not too sure she would have trusted plastic to protect her beloved upholstered furniture.

While thinking about my mother's ritual, I began to apply it to human behavior when meeting someone that we want to impress. It seems to be a natural instinct to 'put on another face' for strangers.

When animals mate they have rituals. Dances, prances and all sorts of showy behavior not common in everyday life in their species. We are not that much different.

Watching my children through their dating years and remembering my own 'dating behavior' I know that the show is on when we are trying to impress. But eventually it is all too much hard work. That is when we really get to know one another, after the cushions have been flipped back to the comfortable side.

If everyone sticks around for the conversion then the relationship just might have a chance.

"So you're looking at your past through a broken glass puzzle of mistakes that you made."©
Emerson Hart

OOPS!

When asked to recall one of the most terrible moments in my career, I had to think for only a second and a moment in time came back like a boomerang to hit me in the most embarrassing memory moments head.

My agent had submitted me to casting director Juliet Taylor for a small part in Wolf a Jack Nicholson film playing his flamboyant author friend. I would only have one scene, but I knew I could ace it.

The morning of the audition, I let my naturally curly

145

hair be it's wild self and I donned a pair of large dangling earrings and morphed into my best artistic flamboyant self. As I entered the elevator to go to the casting directors floor, Ellen Lewis her assistant popped in after me. She took one look at me and her eyes widened in disbelief. Hoping it was not just my imagination, I waited my turn in the outer office. Soon my name was called and I entered Juliette's office.

It seems that she saw my anchor experience on my headshot resume and I was there to audition for a straight, serious anchor person. Not the flamboyant author! I was in such shock that I had taken time to carefully plan to look like someone else than the real me, I couldn't tell her the truth, that I was dressed for another part.

She was kind enough to let me read, while she closed her eyes. Probably trying to imagine that this floozy could pass as an anchorwoman. Looking back, I should have spoken up about the mistake and would have probably gotten the other role, but instead, I just let it go because I was intimidated by her importance in the industry.

The lesson I learned here, is to not let things get out of control and to believe in yourself enough to correct situations when you can.

Poetic justice is that they never used an anchor woman in any scene, so I would have been out of a job anyway.

"If you want to have a good cry, go to the New Jersey DMV and mourn the death of what helped make American strong, our voice of reason."

The Death Of Common Sense

The driver's license that I have held for 35 years in New Jersey was about to expire, but instead of sending payment by mail as I usually do, I was asked to renew in person at the nearest DMV. Another annoyance I thought, but it would be helpful to have a digital license with my picture on it for ID purposes.

There is a 6 point list of ID's one can bring to prove you are who you are. So I brought my passport (4 points), property tax bill and social security card.(2 each, giving me 8 points for good measure). These along with my old driver's license (still valid) should do.

New Jersey is one of the few states that is following a pilot identity system under Homeland Security guidelines to prevent identity theft. In other words, we New Jersey drivers are caught in an experimental nightmare until Big Brother works out the kinks.

Seeing that my passport had my hyphenated married name and that my social security, tax bill and drivers license did not. Never mind that my picture and all other ID matched. I was asked to return with birth certificate and all other name ID I have had since I was born (including marriages).

Okay. Angry, but not one to buck the system, I showed up with 16 points of documentation from birth certificate on. I even brought some books with my picture and name on them. I was really desperate. Not good enough said the three supervisors that were younger than my own children. No one was able to match the dots that were so obvious to a thinking person, I growled under my breath. One marriage certificate had no seal they said. "But look, it's is on official Virginia Government documented paper.!" I said to deaf ears.

I gathered all my paperwork and took it to my local district councilman's office and they vowed to help my, using their contacts in Trenton and the DMV here. I went home and breathed a sigh of relief that I would soon beat the red tape of this confused system that was strangling my ability to drive in my home state.

Wrong! They reported back two days later and said that I either had to change my name, a legal name by the way ,on my social security card and my medicare card (do you know what a nightmare that would be) or change my name on my passport (do you know what another nightmare that would be). I asked the girl on the phone if she had a passport. "No," she replied. "How did you get your driver's license," I asked. 'Birth certificate' was her answer.

That afternoon, I gathered up three pieces of ID, my birth certificate, social security card and marriage license to my late husband plus tax bill to prove that I lived in the State of New Jersey, explaining the 'Hart' part of my name. I *am* Sandra Hart, believe me. I went to a different DMV and within 30 minutes had my new digital driver's license with photo ID and whatever encrypted info was on the card.

They got it. They were able to connect the dots with these few pieces of ID, whereas, the other non-thinking folks couldn't see it with 16 pieces. I realize that driving is a privilege, but has common sense gone out the window by Homeland Security since 9/11?

What Was I Thinking

Faster Than The Speed Of Light

Internet commerce is just wonderful, isn't it? On-line ordering has become de rigueur of my life. The world of shopping for everything I need to exist or to pamper my little heart is just a click away. No need to get into the gas-guzzling SUV, or spend hours going from store to store hair-pulling, pricing, searching until my patience is exhausted. I can sit my pajamas and find the world of shopping dreams in the comfort of my own home. 'Let your fingers do the shopping' has never been truer. But a warning to the wise...be sure you really want that item! I have found that if when ordering, you change your mind within five minutes, you are dead in the water. Not even your demise will cancel your 'Submit Order" request.

I recently had to order a new printer and went on-line to purchase another. Stupid me, in a rush, ordered one that I thought was a good bargain, so I clicked through my order, not thinking fast enough about the forty dollar delivery charge that they sneak in on you at the end. Five minutes later, I changed my mind after I quickly logged on to the HP website and found another with FREE shipping.

Not trusting the web contacts, I called directly to customer service at Target to cancel my five-minute-old order. Someone in Mumbai told me it was too late to cancel. Then someone on a live customer service web chat line identified as Debbie told me it was too late to cancel. No one, live or over the web would change their minds about my order.

I am now stuck with two printers and will have to be glued at home to refuse Target's order that won't even be shipped for three days!

Lesson learned is that keep your mind and fingers on the same 'page' and don't let your fingers do the walking unless your brain says okay.

How Does Your Garden Grow?

Ever since her husband Don died, Julia's flower garden became the most beautiful sight for residents driving up or down our little six-house road. Each spring to the delight of all of us her perky daffodils would be the first to pop their heads above the grape hyacinths and early pansies. Her winter cabbage was still providing color along the border of her meandering walkway. Each season, one after another, didn't disappoint as the wild flowers, perennials and annuals added color to her yard...and our lives, including, obviously, Julia's. As soon as the soil was soft enough to be tended to, she was in her garden coaxing the finest beauty from each of her delicate flora family.

In anticipation of the wonderful burst of color as we passed by Julia's, we always looked forward to that first late spring drive down our road on our way home from our southern snowbird life in Florida.

"What have we here!" we gasped this year. Julia's perennials were there, but in between we could see aggressive weeds poking their ugly heads about her garden. Was Julia not well, or perhaps on a long trip somewhere?

Anxious about her well-being, we knocked at Julia's door and a very radiant and much trimmer Julia answered the door. She was all smiles as she invited us in for coffee and introduced us to her new beau.

The mystery was solved. I realized that Julia had replaced one love for another in her life. I never thought of one's garden as a barometor of one's life, but my next door neighbor has prompted me to rethink that question.

I hope that Julia one day soon will be able to handle two loves in her life at once; her beau *and* her garden. At least before the chrysanthemums are due to bloom again.

"Fantasies belong on the silver screen. When the projector stops the dream is gone."

Affairs Of The Heart

Although I've always lived by a strict moral code, even in my younger years, I never was very good at serious dating because I always neglected to look at the future of the relationship realistically. What I wanted, what I thought I needed, I wanted now. A boyfriend. The future and was way out there. Today was all that mattered. I was I love with love and all the happy endings that filled the movie screens fueled that dream.

It is so easy be blinded by the first passions of a

relationship that close our eyes to realistic thoughts about tomorrow and the honest dynamics of the interactions beyond that initial amore.

I never waited for or sought out relationships that mattered, I always took what came along and if the chemistry was there that was all that mattered. (i.e., if he liked me) I brushed away any immediate realities for fear that no one else was going to come along.

It took a few misfires in my 'modus operandi' to set me straight. I learned not to give my heart away in go-nowhere relationships. When it is right, it will happen and fantasies belong on the silver screen.

What Was I Thinking?

Sometimes I think I don't know who I really am. I have gotten lost in the shuffle of who people *think* I am.

My husband thinks I am a person who has no sense of humor, who doesn't drink and can't 'go with the flow'. Of course he doesn't realize that I am not a salmon who wants to swim up stream with him while everyone else is going the other way.

On the other hand, my children think of me as the expert at giving 'guilt trips'. I haven't a clue what they mean. Really. What is a guilt trip? I wouldn't know one if it hit me in the face.

My grandchildren think of me as their best playmate always ready to give out hugs and kisses, talk on the phone for hours and put their pictures on my screen saver just because I love them. Unconditionally.

Looking in the mirror, the image that I see is closer to what my grandchildren see. I am not perfect, of course, but I don't see in myself some of the qualities that my husband and children do.

Perhaps after all of these years they do not see the real me, or I cannot see the real me. What is the truth? Who am I? Their version or mine?

There is often a conflict in what we perceive about ourselves and what others see. That is why we have wars and divorces and disowning of parents and children.

I have found the best defense is an offense. If you can't beat them, join them. "You are so right, my darlings." Please pass the salt.

Change That Doesn't Jingle

Here on the East Coast a sign that summer is fading is the constant music of the tree cicadas awaking us in the morning and serenading us at night. In spite of this signaling of the beginning of the end of summer, I could think of no better song with which to exit the season.   The chorus of the roaring boats cutting through the water, our New England buoy bell clanging in the breeze and the cicadas. What a symphony!

When one of my children moved to Los Angeles, I walked around with a microphone and taped this chorus to remind them of home. These melodies are the one constant in my life here on the shore that I can count on.

Reality, though, brings each of us other events that are surprises and are certainly more difficult to deal with than the changing of the seasons.

I won a small gold trophy for placing third in the 5K Lance Armstrong Race in South Beach, Florida. A vegetarian, never on medication, always fit and defying my chronological age, I felt invincible.

Then I woke up one morning and could hardly get out of bed. Every muscle and joint in my body ached as if I had done hard labor the day before. Overnight my active life as I had known it disappeared. I was eventually diagnosed with Polymyalgia Rheumatica. PMR is a condition that causes severe morning stiffness, usually affecting women around 50 or older.

The cause of PMR is not known. Some scientists think the illness may be at least partly inherited and others believe that is caused by a virus.

Since it came overnight and I have no history in my family of the disease, I personally suspect a stress-related virus. After two years in 50% of the people it just goes away. I hope that I am in that category.

My purpose in sharing my battle with PMR and my inability to accept a negative change in my life, and to for the first time in my life, not be in control of my health and body, is to touch those of my readers who may also be struggling with change and control in their lives.

Your change may not be health related, but be assured that if you recognize those situations you do have control over, the battle is more than half won. Don't fear change, but think of it as another challenge that will open the door to new directions and strengths.

What Was I Thinking

Which Are You?

A young woman went to her mother and told her about her life, how things were so hard for her. She didn't know how she was going to make it, and she wanted to give up. She was tired of fighting and struggling. It seemed as one of her problems was solved, a new one popped up. Her mother took her into her kitchen, where she filled three pots with water. In the first pot, she placed some carrots, in the second one, she placed some eggs, and in the third pot, she placed some ground coffee beans. She let them sit and boil without saying a word, then in about twenty minutes, she turned off the burners. She fished out the carrots and placed them into a bowl. She pulled the eggs out and placed them into another bowl, then she ladled the coffee yet into another bowl. Turing to her complaining daughter, she asked, , "Tell me what do you see?" "Carrots, eggs, and coffee, " her daughter replied.   She brought her daughter closer, and asked her to feel the carrots. She did, and noticed that they were now soft. She told her daughter to break an egg, which she did, and after removing the shell, she saw that the egg was not hard-boiled. Finally, she told her daughter to sip the coffee. The daughter smiled as she tasted the right flavor, then asked, "What's the point? Her mother explained that each of the three object had faced the very same adversity, boiling water, but each had reacted differently: The carrot want in strong, hard and unrelenting. However, after being subjected to the boiling water, it softened, and became   weak. The egg had been fragile. Its thin outer shell had protected its liquid interior, but after sitting through the boiling water, its insides became hardened.   The ground coffee beans were unique, however. After they were in the boiling water, they had changed the water! "Now which are you?

When adversity knocks on your door, how do you respond? Are you a carrot, an egg, or a coffee bean?

Think of it like this.. Which am I? Am I a carrot that appears to be strong, but with pain and adversity, do I wilt, and become soft and lose my strength?

Am I an egg, that starts out with a malleable heart, but changes with the heat? Did have a fluid spirit, but after a death, a breakup, a financial hardship, or some other trial, have I become hardened and stiff?

Or am I like the coffee bean? The bean actually CHANGES WITH WATER!

What Was I Thinking

(*The following is an excerpt from a speech I gave in 2007*)

Living In The Light

I may be dating myself, but when I was eight I had a perfect plan for my life. I was going to go to Hollywood and marry the handsome movie star and the love of my imaginary life, Gary Cooper. And of course, on top of that I was going to be a famous movie star. Well, as you can guess by my standing here before you, my plans for my young life were not exactly what was mapped out for me. Besides, if my calculations are correct, today Gary Cooper would be 102 and not much of a date at Starbucks or a lifetime partner walking hand and hand with me into the sunset. I had other roads to travel, some wonderful and fulfilling. Others memorable, and those that I that I would not care to re-walk again. Life is made of choices. Coming here today was a choice for you. What you decided to wear, what time you decided to leave. How you got here and what roads to take. Every day from the moment we get up, we have decisions to make about daily living and consequence from those decisions sometimes should be certain, but never are 100 per cent sure. If you take road Y it will get to road X. But, other times the choices we make have consequences that don't give us a clear idea ahead of time of the outcome. The schools we attend, the relationships we enter, the children we chose to have or not have. The logical choices, getting from Y to road X seems so easy…but sometimes don't give the results we expect. The road may be closed, so we have to detour, we may have a flat tire. Logically, and usually, we can depend on these choices to get us to where we want to got, but in life **nothing** is a 'for sure', no matter how much our reason tells us it is.

"Before I knew the sea...I knew the sea inside of me and I knew the feel of sand between my toes and the chilly rush of waves upon my feet. Before I knew the sea...I knew the sea inside of me."

Do You Care?

While walking and enjoying the foamy serf pounding the shore along our ocean boardwalk the other day, I was in animated conversation with a friend ignoring what surrounding chatter was within our peripheral, we were chased by a young woman waving a clip board at us.

Won't these pollsters with a cause ever let us rest, I

thought, trying to ignore her as we continued down the boardwalk. But she was intent on stopping us and soon got her way as we paused to hear her spiel.

"I am with ABC-TV and we are doing a show in which we create disturbances and see how people react. Whether they stop, and get involved, call 911 or just pass by not wanting to get involved. We have both of you on tape and need your permission to use you if we need to."

Obviously, I was more clueless than my friend, who said she saw a disturbance between two women, but it looked like it was resolved, so all she did was make a face toward the women. Naturally, I was the one who didn't even hear so see a thing, so focused was I on my conversation with her. Well, we signed the releases and I walked away with the knowledge that I was not so street smart after all.

Winding up as a non-responsive citizen is quite embarrassing. I now vow to be more aware of my surroundings, not only for my own safety, but that of my neighbors.. It is a crazy world we live in.

Another Chance To Get It Right

How do you handle adversity? I have found that in life we are thrown so many curves that it is impossible to understand which direction will enable us to jump to emotional safety. And why we have made choices that have put us where we are, is a mystery. But my choices lead me to where I am today. I can't honestly say I would do it all over again the same way. But the bottom line for me is that I have taken the bad from my life and have reversed it for the good. I'm sure that if you think back on your life some decisions you have made would have taken you another direction, maybe for the better or worse, but who is to judge that those choices were right or wrong.

My husband's mother, the only girl in a family of 6 boys, came over from Poland at the age of 14 to get away from farm work and to be able to go to school. In Poland at that time only the boys were given a chance to go to get any type of education. When she arrived at Ellis Island her only bag of clothing was stolen and the relatives that were to meet her did not show up. She could have gone to live with relatives in Illinois, but because they were not religious, she chose to stay in New York and work in the garment sweat shops. Life was very tough for the pretty girl with long blond curls that really deserved better. She had a life not of freedom of hard work on the farm, but of sewing for long, long torturous hours for practically only pennies in the dirty sweat shops of lower Manhattan.

She eventually met a young man who was a pants presser and they had four children…her first daughter died at three years of age with a mastoid infection. Fanny's entire life was difficult to the end and in her eyes (and in reality) she had few happy days.

Choices. Had she gone to Illinois, her relative was mayor of his town and eventually owned what was later know as Paramount Studios. Had she gone west to her less religious relatives, Fanny would have been raised in wealth and educated at the finest schools and perhaps because of these comfortable circumstances she would have had more happy days. But to the day she died, she believed practicing her religion was more important to her. And the fact that she professed to never have had a happy day was less important than the work she did for her synagogue.

As she used to say, "That was her lot in her unlucky life." Choices.

In my case, for one, I know I am a more compassionate person because of the trials of my choices and that my career successes have come because of my inner strength that I had to develop for survival. The children and grandchildren that have been such a positive joy in my life would not have been had I not made the choices in my life that I did. These indeed are the most very special gifts that make up for all of the rest of the stuff I have had to wade through.

Life gives us no guarantee that it is going to be as it is the movies, but we can take from it and use our lessons for positive growth forward. Yesterday is truly gone, we have no control of that, but the promise of a new day is real and right in front of us. Isn't life wonderful!! Another chance to get it right.

What Was I Thinking

"The Magnificent Maidens who guarded our city of cities at the point where the ocean and rivers bleed into one another are gone."

A Day Etched In History

Our house sits on the highest point of the Atlantic shoreline and the glistening Sandy Hook Bay gives way to the dark rolling Atlantic beyond the beach. Rising above the ocean swells that God should have reasoned was enough beauty for us humans to savor at one time, and stretching as far as the eye can see, the crown jewels of the Northeast glistened as the new sun set fire to the windowed skyline of New York City. The ability to have this panorama in my life on a daily basis never bores me and I usually don't tale it for granted. But Tuesday was not a usual day.

The phone rang. Why so early, I mumbled to myself. My daughter was on the other end. "Mother, an airplane slammed into the World Trade Center!"

Her words were incredible. Did I hear her right?

'What', I said as I turned toward the ocean, my eyes searching to prove her wrong.

I looked out onto the familiar horizon and billows of dark smoke were erasing the color from the blue sky that stretched along the rest of the city skyline and beyond.

My husband and I watched in disbelief, hardly grasping what we were seeing, when another large billow of smoke erupted like a white silk parachute exploding at full force and lifting vertically into the air.

Our neighbors started coming one by one and we gathered shoulder to shoulder on the deck, each silenced by the enormous spectacle.

Then one by one they dispersed just at quietly as they came and Arthur and I went into the house to watch with the rest of the world the unfolding of the tragic events we had just witnessed.

Six hours later I was back on the deck, still somewhat in shock and starring at unending clouds of death blowing with the afternoon winds northward, trailing high into the sky. The Magnificent Maidens who guarded our city of cities at the point where the ocean and rivers bleed into one another are gone.

Here I was in America, standing on the ocean's edge among the green trees and songbirds. In this bucolic setting, I was watching a war 14 miles away. It was more surreal than anything I could have even imagined I would ever witness. It was unthinkable. It was unbelievable.

Only the steady groan of the large ferries traveling back and forth executing rescue missions between out two shores kept me in reality. This was not just a bad dream. Who would have thought that this could happen here?

I am old enough to remember listening to the radio while cross-legged on the floor when President Franklin Roosevelt died. I was too young to understand the sadness our country felt, but I remember.

I remember that I was feeding my baby when Walter Cronkite told us that John F. Kennedy had been shot, and I cried.

And when Martin Luther King was assassinated I was both saddened and fearful.

Now and forever I will remember that day in

September. I will remember how we here in America died as a result of unspeakable acts of violence against innocent people. Thos who have lost their lives in these tragic terrorist attacks are gone forever. Those of us that have been left behind had lost something that next to life is the most precious thing we possess.

We have lost our ability to take an airplane or go into a building or to walk the streets with out fear of harm. We have lost our ability to feel safe from terrorism in any corner of America and the world. We have lost an important part of our freedom.

I will never forget where I was on September 11, 2001. I will never forget where I was on this horrendous day when deeds of man against man were applauded in the name of religion.

If I were Only Eighteen Again!

I'm in love with the guy who is painting my house. Well, not in a 'Love' love way, but in a sort of "if I were only 18 again" way. When I saw my painter balancing two stories high on a ladder with a paint can held by one finger, I was convinced painting houses was just his hobby. There was no doubt in my mind that on his 'real work' days he was in the ring giving a slam dunk to his WWF opponent. Three men could inhabit his muscular body and there would still be extra room. His biceps are bigger than my husband's waist and the dark hair on his head is even bigger. And the most attractive asset of all, he is young. What more could a woman want I fantasized while loading the dishwasher for the millionth time, my estrogen pill melting on my tongue without water because the dishwasher hose was still attached to the sink faucet. And never mind the henna that was aimlessly dripping down the side of my neck from underneath my shower cap and onto my robe. The Rock, or whatever his name, was painting my house.

What caused me to begin to lose my curly red head, you ask? Well, it all started when my husband sourly suggested he was becoming unnerved by listening to my classical music all day long and immediately put on a couple of rock CD's by his favorite artist, my son. Emerson does create great music, but the soothing sounds of violins and cellos somehow help carry me through mundane tasks of the day.

I've always categorized my life in music phases: The Four Aces, Bill Haley and Elvis represent my adolescent memories; Johnny Mathis, Montavonni, and Peter, Paul and Mary my baby-raising years: Kiss, Springsteen, Buffalo Springfield and anything else my three teenagers played at mega-decibel levels represent my 'whatever' years.

My white-haired husband who had never ever heard of the likes of Mic Jagger or Sting in his life until he met my children, has now become the maven of rock.

And now, this seemingly useless information I've just shared with you about music tastes, segues us back to The Rock who is painting my house. I really didn't fall in "lone not really LOVE" with The Rock. I fell in love with the dichotomy between his physical age and appearance and his taste in music.

All day long, The Rock listens to his portable radio he never has more than five feet away from his ladder. And the music that filters through my windows brings me back to my teenage life. To my amazement, music of the 50's is the music that makes Rock's heart beat. It is his taste in music that I love. And it is his music that makes me feel alive again by sparking anew the excitement of finding teenage love in a time once lived.

When his work is done and The Rock and his radio drive down the road, I'll miss the journey his music has provided. So in the end, I guess it's not all about youth and muscles or The Rock's plentiful hair. And it's not about painting either. It's about comfortable memories and the ability to dream in your fuzzy slippers.

What Was I Thinking

Cherishing The Value Of The Moment

Political writers are a conundrum. They constantly have their tentacles out searching for the truth and researching the facts as presented to them. Yet, they are schooled to rein in, suppress and not let emotions interfere with their work in order to present an unbiased picture of that hallowed truth with their words. Those words are mirrors that help us see.

In the past, as a reporter, I have been schooled to suppress the influences of my feelings in print and on television so often, that perhaps in doing so. My own memories at times were sadly too short. It was a struggle to reverse that pattern of thinking when I ended my journalistic television career years ago and more recently, in the writing of my memoir. In my prior work the facts were the facts and I allowed myself to share nothing in between.

I have always been touched by the writings of syndicated columnist Leonard Pitts of the Miami Herald and his acute observations on modern life. His ability to utilize keen observations and feelings allow us to see with his words the reflection of our own world. He is a good reporter who has the pulse not only on his own feelings, but ours as well.

He, Andy Rooney, the late Charles Kuralt and other masters of observation and opinion have taught me well. I have learned that when my writing poignantly defines and allows me to share a moment in my life with you, I have finally come full circle.

There is no middle, proving that when you cherish the value of a moment in time, you hold it in your hand forever and it can never really be lost. For whatever you carry in your heart is yours to keep always. There may be moments forgotten, but in rediscovering them, old roads can be walked again and that is something very special indeed.

Laughter Is The Language Of Survivors

My cousin Joan in Atlanta sent me an e-mail forward that extols the virtues of senior women vs. the sweet young things we all used to be. It noted it was written by a man in an "Old Fart's Hat."

Well, it was an 'oh, so true' funny piece that made me laugh and I enjoyed it even more because it reminded me of a time several years ago when my husband and I were in an elevator at Caesar's Palace in Atlantic City. The elevator doors opened and in walked a man in a crisp blue baseball hat with "Old Fart" on it. Right behind him trailed his wife (I assume) with her own proud blue baseball cap perched on top of her curly perm heralding that she was the "Old Fart's Wife." I had to bite my tongue to keep from laughing and I elbowed my husband when he started to guffaw.

At the time I thought it pretty funny for people to have the nerve to be walking around like that, they might as well have had dunce caps on their heads, but in hindsight I see how great it actually was. God bless that man and his wife. Only in America could they have the freedom to walk around in public in an "Old Farts" ball cap as an expression of their humor and who they were. In Afghanistan they would have been shot.

The point in all of this is that I don't know how you feel about it, but I need to begin laughing again. I need to find those moments in my life, the pockets of human behavior that tickle me in a way that make me feel alive and part of this wonderful universe.

Years ago I remember reading about the director Josh Logan and his struggle with depression. On a daily basis he watched Laurel and Hardy films and anything else that would make him laugh. Along with medication, he testified with great conviction that laughter helped him get well.

It is a scientific fact that laughter is good medicine for healing and I believe as a nation we all need to start the process of our own recovery by regaining our ability to find guiltless pleasure in our own joy.

It is true that a part of each of us died on September 11th and we will never be able to resurrect that piece, but we can puck up and go on and find other pieces of light in our lives, or else the enemy can claim victory.

So tonight tickle your kids, play a joke on you spouse and rent a funny movie the whole family can enjoy. Laughter is the language of survivors.

What Was I Thinking

Who Are We Kidding?

Ever since I watched the 9/11 disaster from our summer home on the shores of New Jersey, this nervous Nellie has been a bit squeamish about going through the long Lincoln Tunnel that runs under the river from New Jersey and opens into the city. The city that I constantly dreamed of as a child and that has for a long time held my heart, New York. But it finally took nothing stronger than a mother's love to pull me back again to the city of survival. My son was coming to town.

Last Monday we had lunch with him and his band, Tonic, at a little diner in Chelsea near our apartment just north of the Village. The boys were in town for a special event put together for winners of a contest and we were invited to tag along.

That evening we arrived at Le Bar Bat on 57th Street where Arthur and I were quickly ushered in behind the "big red velvet rope" guarded by men with muscles bigger than Arnold's.

When inside the door, we were stamped like a pork rump that has passed FDA inspection. From there a host herded us toward a pretty young woman in a fetching blue wig with a figure to die for who tagged us with Technicolor hospital-like bracelets that would "allow us two free drinks".

She then moved us on to another amazingly handsome young man with the whitest teeth I have ever seen who pinned us with flashing lapel pins that said something I couldn't for the life of me read upside down. It could have said "Big Jerk for Letting This be Pinned on You", for all I knew. He then sent us on to another beautiful girl wearing a pink wig who decked us out in fluorescent blue neck ring. I think she said something about free massages and Tarot card reading, but before I could question my hearing that was altered severely by my rock concert earplugs, we were moved along like a herd of cattle by the swell of enthusiastic Tonic fans behind us.

One would think that after a few years of attending rock concerts and hanging out in the dressing room with kids who are my age divided by three, that I would be used to it by now. But long ago I have given up my pathetic attempts to blend in and not be so obviously, "What is *she* doing here?" The truth is that even the 'clueless' figure out that Arthur and I have to be someone's parents. Trust me, if you ever want to feel your age, just go to a rock concert. It is a humbling experience being with kids who never think they are ever going to be, nor look as old as you.

But in the end there is sweet revenge for old folks like us. While others are tramping through the cold to city garages, or waiting in the chilly night wind for a cab, bus or subway to take them home, life can be sweet for the parents of a rock star. For instance, when your son gives you a lift a 3 a.m. back to your Chelsea apartment in his new bright tour bus that is along as a New York City cross-town block and the color of Christmas. And better than that, when he then drops you smack in front of your canopied door, you know you have a special life.

What if the few bleary-eyed people wandering in the streets at that ungodly hour were scratching their heads at us two tired button-down seniors hopping (actually dragging) out of this crimson machine made to carry only young, hip people. And, okay, what if being supportive of your kid's things kind of makes you seem crazy sometimes. The truth for Arthur and I is that there are no better perks that stepping of a big red bus in the middle of the morning after a great night of forgetting how old you really are. Life just doesn't get better than that!

What Was I Thinking

This book is dedicated to my mother and her never ending faith in her children. May her light ever shine within us.

What Was I Thinking

To order this book and other books by Sandra Hart, just log on to www.sandrahart.net

What Was I Thinking

To subscribe to Sandra Hart's informative free monthly ezine about everyday living, *Read Between My Lines,* log on to her website *www.sandrahart.net* and fill out the 'Free 'n Easy'

What Was I Thinking

**All books by Sandra Hart are carried on
www. amazon.com or can be ordered on-line at
www.sandrahart.net or by writing to or faxing
My Artisansway Press
10 Ballinswood Road Suite 3
Atlantic Highlands, NJ 07716
1-732-796-6916**